THE NEW TESTAMENT

New and powerful life! Miracles happen when your whole life is lived with the Spirit of God!

Alfred Lee

World Power Testimony Books

Published by World Power Testimony Books

National Library Board, Singapore Cataloguing-in-Publication Data

Name : Lee, Chow Tet, author.

Description: The New Testament : new and powerful life! Miracles happen when your whole life is lived with the Spirit of God! / Alfred Lee. | Singapore : World Power Testimony Books, 2015. | pages cm.

Identifiers : OCN 922930467 | ISBN 978-981-09-7312-4 (paperback)

Subject : Bible. New Testament.

Classification: LC Classification BS2330.3 | DDC 225.61 -- dc23

Contents

Introduction

God's Spirit lives in me and commands my body. While fully in control of my own actions, I nevertheless move according to His leading—for He is lively and active in me, moving in supernatural ways in my life.

I shall begin by sharing my testimony in a small way within my own country of Singapore, and progress from there to share with the neighboring Southeast Asian region and eventually the world. In this World Power Testimony book, I will share real-life stories of how the Spirit of God is living in me, actively performing many precious miracles in my life. As the Bible says,

> Don't you realize that your body is the temple of the Holy Spirit, who lives in you and was given to you by God? You do not belong to yourself...
>
> *1 Corinthians 6:19 (NLT)*

Bless your Holy Name, LORD! The Holy Spirit often appears and speaks to me, using common words and objects to communicate with me. God's Spirit lives in me and commands my body. I am fully in control of my physical body; at the same time, the Spirit of God works in me, moving my body in specific ways to communicate messages that He wants to send to me. I will reveal more about this later in this book.

The testimonies in this book are all true, and they have been recorded under the fresh guidance of the Holy Spirit. Dear reader, read on patiently, and I will share with you about the many miracles I have received every day from the kingdom of our Holy God. You are in for an exciting time, as I share real-life stories of miracles and revelations from God.

I desire a deeper and deeper relationship with the Spirit of God every day. Mercy shall follow me. God's Spirit is with me all the days of my life. He uses body gestures to communicate with me daily, and we talk together freely and openly.

God's Spirit is omnipresent and omnipotent. I have experienced the awesome, dynamic, supernatural power of the Holy Spirit in my life. I have witnessed His mighty deeds. I have the greatest experiences of our Holy God's living and lively presence here on earth. The Holy Spirit, Holy God, Spirit of God, LORD, and the angels, they are all with me.

The Holy Spirit is omnipresent, omnipotent and omniscient. He knows all about human beings: what is in their hearts, what they want to do (even before they themselves know it), what they like or don't like. He knows all about their lifestyles and cultures, their ways of talking and acting, and the situations they are facing. He knows which people are out to condemn and destroy others, and the pure evil that is in some human hearts today.

I am filled with awe, realizing how great the Holy Spirit is. He knows everything in advance. He is powerful. He is Almighty God. He has commanded me to write this holy book and to name it *The New Testament*; and I have done so, in obedience to His will for me.

Alfred Lee

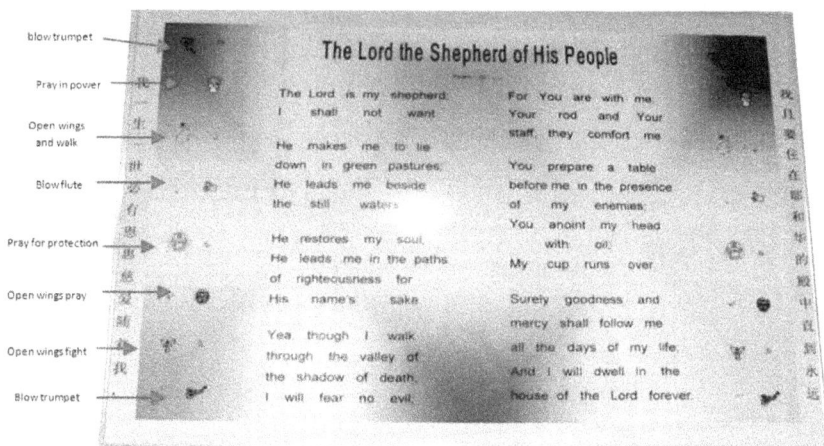

This poster in my living room holds a special significance for me. One day I was at home, feeling scared because of the spiritual warfare going on in my life at the time. The Spirit of God turned my head to face the poster and I saw, floating out of the poster, the words "fear no evil" (from *Psalm 23:4*). Those words were floating on the surface of the poster! I knew it was the Lord speaking to me and assuring me that I need not be afraid because He is my Shepherd and He will always keep me safe.

I had this marble cross made, with the words "Holy presence of God" in English and "Spirit of God Omnipresent, Omnipotent" in Chinese. One day I was facing this cross in my home and looking at the Chinese words on it. I called out, "Spirit of God!" in Chinese, and the Spirit of God appeared to me. God often uses this cross to speak to me.

In the beginning was the Word,
and the Word was with God,
and the Word was God. He was
in the beginning with God. All
things were made through
Him, and without Him nothing
was made that was made. In
Him was life, and the life
was the light of men. And the
light shines in the darkness, and
the darkness did not comprehend it.

John 1:1-5, NKJV

Knowing this first, that no prophecy of
Scripture is of any private interpretation,
for prophecy never came by the will
of man, but holy men of God spoke as
they were moved by the Holy Spirit.

2 Peter 1:20-21, NKJV

A rose to remember our Holy God's voice in the
atmosphere, telling me what to do when I was in
trouble. He appeared many times in my whole life.
Thank you, Holy God, for fighting for us.

Visitors coming for prayer or worship can bring
along a stalk of rose as a symbol of their love for
God, as they draw closer to the Spirit of God.

CHAPTER 1

Miracles of Supernatural Healing and Protection

I did not know how to pray in ordinary words, but the Holy Spirit taught me how to pray in tongues. Powerful! I prayed in the Spirit with supernatural power. I engaged in spiritual warfare, and I received healing and protection from the LORD. Explaining to me how to pray in tongues, the Holy Spirit said, "Think about what you want to pray."

As the Holy Spirit prayed together with me, the numbness in my hand was gone. My leg cramps disappeared. My fingers stopped feeling itchy. I held a dying man in my arms and prayed in tongues over him. He recovered and got up, looking energized. He looked very much alive and said I had a bright future ahead of me. I prayed with another man, a non-believer, and he too began to speak in tongues.

One morning, the Holy Spirit told me to visit my mother. She had a swollen leg and, as I prayed for her, God healed her. Until the day she went home to be with the Lord, her leg was fine; she had no more problems with it. Truly, God works just as powerfully through ordinary Christians like me, as He does through His pastors; He makes no distinction between us.

Many times, the Spirit of God would waken me up at midnight to pray. Each time, as I prayed in tongues, God made my tongue roll supernaturally. One night He woke me up to pray for my church leader, who was suffering from a pain in his hand. I prayed in tongues for his healing but, after praying, I was still worried about him. Then the Holy Spirit assured me that he had been healed, and indeed he was. On another occasion, the Spirit of God woke me up at midnight and healed me of a pain in my tongue.

The Spirit of God is so good to me! Whenever I slip on the pavement or road, I feel there is someone behind me, supporting my back, so that I do not fall. Once, while I was at home writing my testimony, I fell suddenly from my chair onto the floor. There was no reason for this to happen, as the chair was in good condition and I was sitting quietly in it. The chair landed upside down on the floor but I was totally unhurt. I had felt a supernatural power breaking my fall as I landed very lightly and safely on the floor.

The Holy Spirit often tells me to reduce the speed of my motorbike when I am going too fast, so that I will not get into an accident. Once, while I was riding my motorbike, one of my hands became very numb. That put me in grave danger, as I could not properly handle my bike with only one hand. The Spirit of God told me to pray in tongues. I obeyed, and the numbness left my hand. Praise the Lord!

One day, when I was worshipping in church, my legs went numb and I collapsed onto the floor. I said in my heart to the Spirit, "No matter what happens to me, whether I am paralyzed or in a wheelchair, I am not afraid, for you are with me." Immediately, the numbness left my legs and I could walk.

On another occasion, the Holy Spirit spoke to me. He said, "Hot Soup"; that was His way of telling me there was a problem. A few days later, I felt a pain in the upper part of my back. The Holy Spirit told me to pray, and I did. The pain went away. I suffer from this kind of back pain occasionally, and it is always a manifestation of spiritual battles happening around me. The pain is a signal from the Holy Spirit to pray and engage in spiritual warfare.

Another time, the Angel of the Lord was beside me and I heard a voice calling me to fast (the voice sounded like a lady's voice). I obeyed, even though it meant that I had to miss my breakfast. For one whole year, I skipped breakfast and fasted in the mornings. Before that, I used to take a late breakfast and I would feel very sick after eating the food. But, after that one year of fasting, when I resumed taking my breakfast, I found that I had been healed of my after-breakfast sickness. Nowadays, I can take my breakfast at any time and I feel well throughout the day. Praise our Holy God!

Without the Holy Spirit, I can do nothing. He often informs me about big spiritual battles ahead. He helps me pray so that I can be covered by His protection over me. The Holy Spirit teaches me and holds my hand so that I can walk safely. He sharpens my spiritual senses so that I can detect and avoid danger.

The greatest thing in life is to know Jesus Christ. Every day I give thanks in prayer to the LORD for His protection and healing, His grace and favor, His mercy and goodness, and His many blessings. I thank Him for the holy wisdom I have received from Him and for His constant presence in my life. I rejoice that I will dwell in the house of the LORD forever.

CHAPTER 2

Miracles of Financial Blessings and Provision from Our Holy God

*B*efore I became a Christian many years ago, I made a deal with God: I told Him that, if He would help me set up a successful business, I would accept Christ. I then proceeded to start a courier service, although I did not know anything about doing business. We soon got into difficulties. We did not even have a single client. Then I received an idea from God — to fax advertisements to potential clients, telling them about our business. Soon all four of our phones started ringing and we had more clients than we could handle. That was the end of poverty for us; we had received abundant financial blessings from our Heavenly Father.

The Holy Spirit knows everything that is going to happen in the future. We should always listen to Him. One day, the only delivery man we employed in our courier business didn't turn up for work. He called and gave excuses as to why he couldn't come that day. This put us in a tight spot, as there were urgent deliveries to be made. There and then, I decided to look for another deliveryman but my wife objected to it. The Holy Spirit told me to go ahead and fight for it. So I quickly went and got a new deliveryman—and thank God I did, because the old one played us out; he never came back to work. Imagine what would have happened if I had not listened to the Holy Spirit but to my wife instead? We would have been in hot soup with our clients if we hadn't delivered the parcels on time!

Another occasion when God blessed me financially was when I wanted to sell my box van. The Spirit of God directed me to a name card in the van. The card was turned face downwards and I could not see the name on it; yet I sensed that was the dealer I was meant to call. I called him and ended up selling the van to him at a very high price. Praise God!

The LORD is forever in my life. Suddenly I am free of burdens and worries; God by His supernatural power has set my spirit free. My children have all completed their studies and I am ready to retire from my business. God told me to pass the business to the next generation. At first I thought about my sons; but then the Holy Spirit prompted me to give room to my daughters. My retirement plan is to serve the Lord. I desire to plant churches and see the whole nation of Singapore worship our Holy God.

God has blessed me so much in my life, even before I came to know Him. My wife grew up in a village. She had some education and stayed home to take care of the children in their younger days. At the time, I had not come to know the Lord. I started my courier business without any money, education or experience. I had no knowledge of the trade, nor did I receive support from anyone. I wanted my business to succeed; I wanted a truck with my business name on it; I wanted all my children to make it to the university.

I got it all—a truck, a successful business, and all my three children are university graduates. I am indeed blessed. I asked, "Why?" The Spirit of God replied that, even before I knew Him, He was already looking after me. The Lord Almighty cares for the poor and weak (like I was); He wants to pour out His abundant grace and mercy, holy wisdom, and protection on them.

The Holy Spirit cares for me. True! I used to bring a 500ml water bottle to work, but the Holy Spirit told me to take a 1.5 liter bottle instead. I did as He instructed and found that indeed the bigger bottle served me better. The Spirit of God often tells me to take healthy food and to drink carrot juice and hot tea. He also reminds me to cut my hair whenever it gets too long. The Holy Spirit knows our every need. He knows what we will need in the present and in the future.

The whole world is asking, "Where is God?" In answer to this question, I want to testify that God is with you all the time. Whenever you face difficulties, He is there for you. Whenever you are in trouble, the Holy Spirit will show up to help you. He will manifest His "super" power in your life. He is invincible. Everything He does is done superbly, magnificently, wonderfully. This is the truth. This is what I have experienced in my life for many years now.

I am very appreciative of all the Holy Spirit has done for me, and amazed and awed by His faithfulness and goodness. Everything He has done for me is done "sharp"—that is, powerfully and perfectly. Everything He told me would happen has come to pass; His predictions of future events have been 100 percent accurate!

CHAPTER 3

God Puts a Song in My Heart Every Day: the Joys of Being His Close Friend

On 14 April 2014, I woke up at 3am with a song in my heart. It sounded like someone was worshipping in me. Then I heard the Spirit of God say, "The Holy Spirit is blessing you."

The Holy Spirit sings in me. Many times I hear worship songs in my heart, and each time it is a different song. Like this one:

"I am a friend of God,
I am a friend of God.
Holy God calls me friend."

Once, unknown to me, mosquitoes were breeding in a glass of water left unattended in my home. The Holy Spirit told me about the mosquito larvae in the glass, and I quickly got rid of the water. If He had not alerted me, the larvae could have grown into mosquitoes that might have spread dengue fever to people in my home and neighborhood.

On another occasion, I needed to hook something onto a wall in my home. I was about to knock a hole in the wall, so that I could put the hook in; but the Spirit of God showed me a small hole that was already there in the wall. It was just the right size for my hook too! Certainly, He knows everything, even down to the tiniest little hole in my home.

One day, while I was in a Christian bookshop, the Holy Spirit directed me to a calendar on display in the shop. The calendar had big, bold Chinese words on it and smaller words in English. The Holy Spirit kept on prompting me to read the small print on the calendar, which I discovered were bible verses written in English. This is what I read:

"Blessed are the poor in spirit,
For theirs is the kingdom of heaven.
Blessed are those who mourn,
For they shall be comforted.
Blessed are the meek,
For they shall inherit the earth.

Blessed are those who hunger and thirst for righteousness,

For they shall be filled.

Blessed are the merciful,

For they shall obtain mercy.

Blessed are the pure in heart,

For they shall see God.

Blessed are the peacemakers,

For they shall be called sons of God.

Blessed are those who are persecuted for righteousness' sake,

For theirs is the kingdom of heaven.

Matthew 5: 3-10 (NKJV)

I bought the calendar and brought it home with me. Since then, the Holy Spirit has spoken to me every day through these bible verses, and they have been a blessing to me in my walk of faith with the Lord.

The Lord has also spoken powerfully to me to abide in His presence and in His Word. As it says in the Bible, unless we abide in Him, we are nothing and we can do nothing by ourselves.

Abide in Me, and I in you. As the branch cannot bear fruit of itself, unless it abides in the vine, neither can you, unless you abide in Me.

I am the vine, you are the branches. He who abides in Me, and I in him, bears much fruit; for without Me you can do nothing. If anyone does not abide in Me, he is cast out as a branch and is withered; and they gather them and throw them into the fire, and they are burned.

If you abide in Me, and My words abide in you, you will ask what you desire, and it shall be done for you. By this My Father is glorified, that you bear much fruit; so you will be My disciples.

As the Father loved Me, I also have loved you; abide in My love. If you keep My commandments, you will abide in My love, just as I have kept My Father's commandments and abide in His love.

These things I have spoken to you, that My joy may remain in you, and that your joy may be full. If you abide in Me, and My words abide in you, you will ask what you desire, and it shall be done for you.

John 15:4-11 (NKJV)

Who will be with me to face the darkest valley of trouble (*Psalm 23:4*)? Nobody; only you, LORD. Thank you very much, Lord Almighty. Though I may not understand all the plans you have for me, I know that my life is in your hands; and through the eyes of faith, I can clearly see that you are good all the time. I am sorry to see the body of Christ split into so many different denominations today; but praise God that we all worship the same Holy God, Jesus.

Jesus, you are my shepherd, you are my Lord, and you are my Holy God. Nothing compares to your promises. I put my trust in you, you are my Savior and my healer. Lord, I offer my life to you as a living sacrifice. Lord, there is none like you. I sing for joy at the works of your hands.

I heard a preacher on the internet saying that blessings are already given to us. How true! I have already received many blessings from God. Everything I have is from our Holy God. I did not know anything to begin with, but I have received holy wisdom from God.

I visited a church and heard the preacher say, "Where do you want to go? Go to God when you face the prospect of walking through the valley of the shadow of death." Yes, indeed, the Spirit of God gives us rest and peace. I stand wholeheartedly for the LORD our Holy God.

CHAPTER 4

Win Spiritual Wars with Praise and Worship Songs

The Spirit of God leads me to talk heart-to-heart with my Heavenly Father. He leads me to win spiritual battles when I sing praise and worship songs. The whole day long, I have peace in my heart as God's Spirit worships together with me. I lift up my hands and my heart to honor and worship the Lord because our Holy God's words are true.

On one occasion, I was facing some challenges and took the day off from work to seek the Lord. I was at home in my bedroom the whole day, listening to the praise and worship songs being played on my CD. As I sang along, praising and worshiping the Lord, I could sense the holy presence of God in my home. The Spirit of God

---

assured me that my family members would be protected by Him.

The Holy Spirit revealed to me that there was "war + war" going on—meaning that there were waves after waves of spiritual warfare, with new wars added to the old ones, and with wars happening both in the spiritual realm and natural realm. However, the Holy Spirit assured me that He would handle this "war + war" and lead me into battle. The Holy Spirit would plan a path for my future. He assured me that God had a plan for my life, and He would turn things around for me. I knew that what the Holy Spirit had empowered would happen and what He had promised would come true.

I began listening to sermons on the internet, to strengthen myself spiritually and to prepare for the "war + war" that the Holy Spirit had told me about. I received holy wisdom from our Holy God. The Holy Spirit was doing all the planning for this spiritual warfare and I knew He would handle everything for me. The Holy Spirit is super-powerful and invincible.

For many years, my master bedroom was dim at night, even with the light on. This was because the only light in there was from a low-wattage bulb. Then, on the very first day when the "war + war" spiritual warfare began, the bulb blew. The Spirit of God, by His supernatural power, destroyed the bulb before my very eyes. I heard a crackling sound and the light went out—just like that! So, I was forced to change the bulb and, this time round, I installed a much brighter light.

The Spirit of God had to destroy the low-wattage bulb because, otherwise, I would not have changed it to a brighter light—and I needed the brighter light to be able to read the song sheets so that I could sing along with the worship songs on the CD. This would help prepare me for spiritual warfare.

One night, the Spirit of God said to me, "Fear no evil"; these words were meant to prepare me to face an impending danger. As midnight approached, my body began shaking as I sensed an evil presence in the room. I kept shouting out "fear no evil" many times, until the evil spirit was gone and my body had stopped shaking.

On another night, I saw a light strike down like lightning from heaven onto a wall of my home. It was the Holy Spirit releasing His divine power into my situation at the time. He spoke to me, telling me to receive power from God, and I knew that surely our Holy God would empower me. As it says in the Bible:

> "But you shall receive power when the Holy Spirit
> has come upon you; and you shall be witnesses to
> Me in Jerusalem, and in all Judea and Samaria, and
> to the end of the earth."
>
> *Acts 1:8 (NKJV)*

I know I belong to you, O Holy God! I know your Spirit sets me free. I do not fight alone but together with the Holy Spirit. The Holy Spirit is in command of my life and makes the best decisions for me. Those who were against me, I have forgotten all about them; but the Holy Spirit takes action on my behalf; the Holy Spirit is my Avenger.

At times, several people would come to me and point to me and start making negative remarks about me. But they soon shut up because God tightens His hold on them to stop them from talking or acting against me. Somehow, they can't think of what to say next (as we say in Singapore, they become "blur"), and so I end up being the one doing all the talking!

Blessed be the name of the LORD. His supernatural power saves, heals and protects us. His supernatural power is at work to deliver us from seemingly hopeless situations and to walk with us through the valley of the shadow of death. His supernatural power sharpens our ears to hear and to understand. His supernatural power gives us grace and rest.

CHAPTER 5

God Speaks to Me in Supernatural Ways

For many years, I listened to Chinese worship songs on a CD—especially one song (我心旋律 or "Melody of My Heart" in English), which touched me deeply. Solemn tears would well up in my eyes, I would cry out, and my whole body would shake as I listened to this song. It was only much later that I realized the lyrics of the song were taken from *Psalm 23* in the Bible. It was just so miraculous and amazing, because the words of the Psalm and the lyrics of the song reflected so truly and accurately the story of my life.

I had a large poster made, with this Psalm on it and with the heading, *The Lord the Shepherd of His People*. This heading, too, was given to me by the Spirit of God. (A picture of the poster is shown on page 4 of this book.)

This poster, which I have displayed prominently in my living room, holds a special significance for me. One day I was at home in my living room, feeling scared because of the spiritual warfare going on in my life. As I fearfully lifted my hand to touch my face, the Spirit of God turned my head to face the poster. All of a sudden, I saw words floating out of the poster in a supernatural way—the words "fear no evil" (*Psalm 23:4*) were floating on the surface of the poster! I knew it was the Lord speaking to me and assuring me that I need not be afraid because He is my Shepherd and He will always keep me safe.

The Spirit of God has also used the poster to communicate with me on many other occasions. For example, He has commanded me to add the words "The Lord the Shepherd of His People" (from the poster heading) and "His name's sake" (from *Psalm 23:3*) to my testimony; that is, this book is written for His name's sake, to glorify the name of our Lord, the Shepherd of His people.

Surrounding the words of *Psalm 23* on this poster are images of angels engaged in spiritual warfare with supernatural power: there are angels praying and releasing their power; angels blowing trumpets in heaven and on earth; angels blowing flutes; angels opening their wings for prayer; and angels opening their wings to fight the enemy.

These images are not merely pictures; God has opened my spiritual eyes many times to see that there are really such angels in the spirit realm.

The Spirit of God placed my finger in my ear; this meant that He wanted me to continue listening to worship songs as I was writing this book. I was listening to the CD as it played the song, "God Will Make a Way"—how apt! I continued to listen to the rest of the songs; the whole CD was full of worship songs! Thank you very much, Spirit of God, for leading me to this marvelous CD that contained such inspiring songs:

> We give You glory, we give you honor,
> We give You everything we are;
> Lifting our hearts and hands before You...
> *From "We Give You Glory" by Don Moen*

Once when I was in bed, the Holy Spirit made my body itch all over so that I could not get to sleep. So I got up and began looking online for sermons. I chanced upon a pastor preaching about praying in tongues—exactly what I wanted to know about at the time! The Spirit of God said that this sermon was for me, and He moved my hand to dig my ear (which meant that He wanted me to listen attentively to the sermon). He said to me, "Holy Spirit"; meaning that this sermon was from the Holy Spirit. Anyone who wants to know about the goodness of praying in tongues should listen to this sermon; simply click on this video link: http://tiny.cc/trinity sermon 22jun14.

Whenever I switch on my computer to listen to preachers on the internet, God would lead me to the sermons or testimonies He wants me to watch. He would also guide me to take down notes all the way throughout the sermon. The Spirit of God would also instruct me as to what kind of sermon it is, and He would categorize the sermons into their respective ministries. And whenever a preacher preaches powerfully and seriously abides in God's Word, the Holy Spirit would tell me that that particular preacher has the Holy Spirit in him and "no running dog"—meaning that he is no sycophant and has no hidden agenda, but is someone who speaks the truth.

The Spirit of God doesn't like "running dogs". Many times, He would point to a "No Dogs Allowed" sign He was showing me. What He meant was that He wanted me to "get rid of the running dogs"—that is, the evil men who were influencing me at that point in my life. It was part of the preparation for spiritual warfare at the time. God's Spirit continued to call out to me, "Get rid of the running dogs." The Spirit of God said, "This is Holy God's rice bowl"— meaning, this matter is very important to God. So I obeyed.

The Spirit of God kept on teaching me from God's Word. When He first started talking to me about the Scriptures,

I couldn't understand much of what He said. But He still continued to talk to me and teach me.

The Holy Spirit acts in His supernatural power to get my mind to dwell often on the Bible. By His power, I keep chewing on God's Word—just like the animals chewing the cud (*Deuteronomy 14:6*). As it says in the Bible:

> Let the word of Christ dwell in you richly in all wisdom, teaching and admonishing one another in psalms and hymns and spiritual songs, singing with grace in your hearts to the Lord.
>
> *Colossians 3:16 (NKJV)*

Without the Holy Spirit, I would not be able to do anything. But He enables me to do everything that He calls me to do. As it says in the Bible:

> I can do all things through Christ who strengthens me.
>
> *Philippians 4:13 (NKJV)*

CHAPTER 6

God Cares for Me through All the Seasons of My Life

here was a period in my life when the Holy Spirit was not present. I had no urge to lift my hands or my heart in worship. I looked around at the congregation and wondered why they were not on fire for God. I had no patience to stay long in that church. After leaving, I began visiting other churches. But I was worried and desperate as I could not fit in. Then I attended a service at a charismatic church and, when I went back home, God told me, "This is your church." I joined this church and liked it.

One day I went to the coffee shop to get my morning cup of coffee but, before I could enjoy it, I heard God saying, "Fast!" Immediately, I obeyed Him and threw away the coffee. Then I began to fear that I would weaken and fall sick because I had missed my breakfast; but there was no need to fear because I continued to enjoy good health from God. In fact, the Holy Spirit goes everywhere with me and strengthens me in my work.

The Spirit of God makes me lie down in green pastures. The Spirit of God leads me beside still waters. Once, when I was worshipping in church, I found that I could not sing anymore because I had sung until my mouth was dry. But the Holy Spirit came to my help—suddenly I found my mouth wet again with saliva (express delivery by the supernatural power of the Holy Spirit!) and I could continue singing! Certainly, the Holy Spirit wanted me to continue praising and worshipping God!

God cares for me, even to the smallest details in my life. I used to suffer from back pain and God healed me; but every now and then I would get a relapse and once, while I was bathing, I asked God "Why?" The Spirit of God told me that it was to stop me from carrying heavy weights that would further injure my back. Sometimes, too, when I had a backache and did not apply a *Salonpas* pain-relieving patch to my back, God's Spirit would move my hand to scratch my back to tell me to put it on.

I wanted to make plans to contribute some money to the support of my mother; but the Holy Spirit told me to hold on first. I did not know why at the time. A few months later, she went home to be with the Lord. The Holy Spirit knew in advance what was going to happen to my mother, and that there was no need for me to make those arrangements for her support.

One morning, as I was getting ready for work, I heard God's voice saying, "Alone, alone, alone." At the time, I did not know why He said that. It took me more than ten years to find out why. I now understand that it was because He did not want me to associate with the evil people who were around me at the time.

The LORD is good all the time. Everything that has happened to me in my life was planned by God, although I may not understand why. I asked Him why it seemed as if I was living under a curse (because I often felt alone in life). The Holy Spirit replied that He had a purpose for everything that had happened in my life. I understood and highly praised the LORD!

Thank you, LORD. Glory to the LORD. I give all to you, LORD. My life is in you, LORD. Holy is the LORD. I will bless your name; I just want to thank you, LORD.

CHAPTER 7

A Message from the Spirit of God to All Christians

*D*ear Christians, please love the Spirit of God first, and then His power — not the other way around. Your love will touch Him to tears. Thank you very much.

The Holy Spirit said to me that those who are "sharp" (that is, those who are sensitive to His presence and leading; those who seek after deeper knowledge and understanding of Him), and who acknowledge Him, touch God's Spirit to tears. The Spirit of God is happy when people honor Him with the praise that is due to Him.

When I am in the presence of the Holy Spirit, I am moved to tears. The Spirit of God opens my eyes to see things unseen by human eyes: angels coming down from heaven, and spiritual beings in the earth's atmosphere. I have seen all these through the supernatural power of the Holy Spirit. Dear reader, you too can experience the power of God's Spirit in your life—very dynamic supernatural power! There are no words to describe it. Just have simple faith and believe that all things are possible with God. Just listen to the Holy Spirit. His words are true.

You must obey the Holy Spirit. In the beginning, as you live your life in this new way, in tune with the Holy Spirit, you might find it strange and different from your old way of life. But please press on; continue to live this new life in the Spirit, and everything will work out fine in the long run. You will be surprised at how you start to look at the world from a different perspective.

You will begin to see with new spiritual eyes, and God will reveal His secrets to you. Keep your mind on the things of God. Chew and meditate on His Word. You will like it very much. It is very precious. Persevere and the Holy Spirit will help you, for the battle belongs to the Lord.

> "So do not fear, for I am with you;
>   do not be dismayed, for I am your God.
> I will strengthen you and help you;
> I will uphold you with my
> righteous right hand."
>
> *Isaiah 41:10*

Jesus said, "I am the Way and the Truth and the Life." (*John 14:6, AMP*) I can testify that this is really true. I have witnessed His acts of supernatural power that you can't find anywhere else on Earth. Truly I tell you, dear reader, that our Holy God is real and living, and He is God of heaven and earth. At the beginning of my Christian life, I wanted to know more about God. I received healing, protection, holy wisdom, grace, and many blessings and miracles from God. I felt the close presence of Almighty God. All this happened in real life—my life!

God is faithful and He will supply all your needs. Dear Christian reader, I have good news for you: the Spirit of God is in you, and He wants to open Himself up to you and talk with you, just as He has with me. I have received powerful revelations from the Holy Spirit. My spirit is open to the Holy Spirit and we communicate with each other. The Spirit of God has shown me many things, clearly and powerfully; there is no limit to the wonders He continues to reveal to me, all in His own timing.

The Holy Spirit has cared for me ever since I accepted the Lord as my Savior. I wanted to know how I could serve Him, and He revealed to me new spiritual insights and opened my eyes to see things unseen by physical eyes. He led me to record the testimonies within these pages; in fact, this book came about as a result of my face-to-face encounters with the Holy Spirit. He commanded me to write it. He called it His "rice cooker" (that was His way of telling me that it was important to Him).

Brothers and Sisters, please help to tell people around the world about this book. If you have been touched or blessed by what is written in these pages, please share it with others, for His name's sake and for the purpose of bringing people to the Lord. From beginning to end, this book contains an important message from the Holy Spirit to the world.

The whole world needs the Holy Spirit. Within these pages are true eye-witness accounts and real-life proofs of how, when we open ourselves fully to God, the Spirit of God will be lively and active in our lives. We will see many miracles happening. Let us shine for Jesus. Let us make a difference in this world for the sake of our LORD. Thank you, dear reader.

> Then Jesus… said, "All authority in heaven and on earth has been given to me. Therefore go and make disciples of all nations, baptizing them in the name of the Father and of the Son and of the Holy Spirit, and teaching them to obey everything I have commanded you. And surely I am with you always, to the very end of the age."
>
> *Matthew 28: 18-20 (NIV)*

The Spirit of God gave me a vision of God disappearing into the water, causing waves to ripple and spread out. The spreading out of the waves represents the Gospel being shared freely and openly throughout the world.

> Love the LORD your God with all your heart, with
> all your soul, and with all your might.
>
> *Deuteronomy 6:5 (NKJV)*

Love the LORD your God with all your heart and with all your soul and with all your mind and with all your strength. You must get rid of whatever idols are in your life, for how else can you draw close to God? How can God have any harmony with an idol? No way, for He is a Holy God. As it says in the Bible:

> How can light live with darkness? And what
> harmony can there be between Christ and the
> devil? How can a Christian be a partner with one
> who doesn't believe? And what union can there be
> between God's temple and idols?
>
> For you are God's temple, the home of the
> living God, and God has said of you, "I will live
> in them and walk among them, and I will be their
> God and they shall be my people."
>
> *2 Corinthians 6: 14-16 (TLB)*

Everything I do is for our Holy God, to our Holy God, with our Holy God, from our Holy God, and through our Holy God. Whatever I do, doing it with God makes all the difference.

> Therefore, whether you eat or drink, or whatever
> you do, do all to the glory of God.
>
> *1 Corinthians 10:31 (NKJV)*

People tell me that I am a "nobody"; but I have the Spirit of God in my heart, and no one is greater than our Holy God. So, in God I am somebody, and I will continue to write testimonies that glorify God and bring His message of love and salvation to the whole world. As it says in the Bible:

> "I know your deeds. See, I have placed before you
> an open door that no one can shut. I know that you
> have little strength, yet you have kept my word and
> have not denied my name."
>
> *Revelation 3:8 (NIV)*

Thank you, Lord, for all your blessings. God directs my path and my life journey. He leads me to fulfill His plans for me and to do His will here on earth, by sharing my testimony around the world so that the whole world will praise the Lord.

God's promises in the Bible have come to pass in my life; everything in the Bible is true. I cherish the precious words of God and His holy presence in my life. As it says in the Book of Isaiah:

> For I am God—I only—and there is no other like me who can tell you what is going to happen. All I say will come to pass, for I do whatever I wish.
>
> *Isaiah 46: 9-10 (TLB)*

The Holy Spirit strengthens me and releases His supreme power to enable me to accomplish God's purposes for me. As it says in His Word:

> But those who wait on the Lord
> Shall renew their strength;
> They shall mount up with wings like eagles,
> They shall run and not be weary,
> They shall walk and not faint.
>
> *Isaiah 40:31 (NKJV)*

The Holy Spirit has called me to open my "wings" for spiritual battles and to fight to defend the Gospel. He has called me to open my "wings" for prayer. He has called me to open my "wings" to "shoot" with tears alone (meaning: to speak out strongly and boldly) with angels helping me, and for the cause of justice; and the Holy Spirit has said that, when I do so, God will promote me and I will arise.

> Arise, my people! Let your light shine for all the nations to see! For the glory of the Lord is streaming from you.
>
> *Isaiah 60:1 (TLB)*

I heard, out of the air, and received from our Holy God, the word, "begging". I felt very sad, as the tears of the LORD came into my eyes. My heart is begging to see the nations worship you, LORD! My heart is begging to serve you more. My heart is begging to know you more, for the sake of your people. My heart is begging to write more for you. My heart is begging that, in the darkness, we can see the Light.

My heart is begging and hoping that you, dear reader, will receive blessings, anointing and knowledge from God; that you will be touched by Him and be sensitive to His holy words; that God will set you on fire for Him, and that you will rise up for Him and start sharing the Gospel "sharp" (that is, in every excellent way) with people around you. As Jesus said in His Word:

> "If you cling to your life, you will lose it; but if you give it up for me, you will save it."
>
> *Matthew 10:39 (TLB)*

CHAPTER 8

God's Heartbeat:
His Call to Plant a Church

God cares deeply about what is happening in the world today. I had stopped listening to the news on the radio; but the Spirit of God commanded me to resume listening, so that I would know what was going on in the world.

Then, one night, as I lay on my bed, God supernaturally turned my head around (one big round, and I didn't do it of my own volition) so that I could see how the electrical wiring track went all the way up to the ceiling in my bedroom. That was a bit scary.

Then I heard God's Spirit speaking to me: "All the tracks go into the cupboard—long and short, all to hang in there." He had shown me the wiring track first, because that was His way of bringing to my mind the MRT (Mass

Rapid Transit) tracks, which at that time were often broken down. He meant that the broken tracks represented the life journeys of people with broken lives. People from all walks of life—whether "long" or "short" types—had their lives hanging in disorder, much like the broken-down tracks.

I have always wanted to plant a church, to reach out to the unsaved people with broken lives. At an early stage of my Christian walk, when I first received my salvation, my church leader (at the time) asked me, "How do you want to serve the Lord?"

I replied, "I want to plant a church."

My leader said, "Tell me that in the future."

Ten years later, I received a call (through a vision) from our Holy God to plant a church. But because I felt inadequate, I rejected the vision. My excuses were that I was "unable" because I was "too old" by then, and besides I saw no way to accomplish the task.

However, the vision appeared again, calling me to plant a church. The Spirit of God assured me that He would make a way. I received holy wisdom from our Holy God to start a ministry for tourists and foreigners coming from all over the world to Singapore. The Holy Spirit encourages visitors to my church to worship the LORD daily during office hours.

I received another vision from the Spirit of God: that those in darkness would see the Light—that is, they would see God. As it says in the Bible:

> "[O]pen their eyes, in order to turn them **from darkness to light**, and from the power of Satan to God, that they may receive forgiveness of sins and an inheritance among those who are sanctified by faith in Me."
>
> *Acts 26:18 (NKJV)*

In my vision, I saw lighted candles. I received our Holy God's command, that it was His will for me to have lighted-up candles in the church I was to plant, which would be called the Spirit of God Christian Church. I welcome everyone to worship the LORD daily during office hours at this church. My purpose is to lead people to Christ.

Nothing is impossible for the LORD. As I obeyed His command to offer my tithes to the church, I was amazed at the many miracles I was receiving from Him. I also received holy wisdom from God to use the tithes to print this book and to utilize the profits from the sales of the book to plant the church. I received revelations from God, too, that it was His plan for the church to start a ministry for tourists and foreign workers; and to call from among them certain people who could serve in the church as helpers.

The church is the greatest holy place of worship. When I was called to plant the Spirit of God Christian Church, I received specific instructions from our Holy God regarding the physical arrangements and design of the church. As I mentioned earlier, I had received a vision of candles in the church; so, in obedience to God's will and command, there will be candles lighted up during church services. I will also be installing a marble cross that holds a special significance for me. I will talk more about this cross later, in Chapter 10 of this book.

I intend this to be a church that will bow down in unison to pray to the Lord. As it says in the Bible, "God is spirit, and his worshippers must worship in the Spirit and in truth." (John 4:24) For the one we worship is a living God who is present among us and is moving actively on earth to fulfil His kingdom purposes. The Holy Spirit, Spirit of God, Holy Lord and His angels are with me. Our Holy God knows the past, present and future: everything we have ever done or will do. My heart was aching and my spirit was in pain, as God convicted me about my past sins. But the Holy Spirit constantly reminds me that I am blessed by God. Hallelujah!

I heard the voice of God saying to me: "Research", "Alone, alone, alone", "This is your church", and "Fast". Our Holy God is real, living, supernatural and powerful. He is LORD Almighty. The Spirit of God knows everything, down to the very littlest detail. I did not know how to write or read, how to read the Bible or pray; but I learnt the Gospel directly from the Holy Spirit and received from Him knowledge that cannot be found in textbooks. He talked to me about many things and gave me insights into people's behavior. As it says in the Bible,

"Silver or gold I do not have, but what I do have I give you. In the name of Jesus Christ of Nazareth..."

Acts 3:6

I received holy wisdom and specific instructions from God, telling me how to set up the Spirit of God Christian Church: the rules and regulations governing the way the church would be run; how He wanted the church services to be conducted; the kinds of ministries the church would have; the people who would make up the congregation; the pastors and preachers who would minister to these people; the place of worship; the physical arrangements and design of the church; and the acceptable ways to obtain funds for the church, one of which would be through the publication and sales of this book.

All profits from the sales of this book will go to the Spirit of God Christian Church Fund. This is how the church will be financially supported, as God has commanded me not to accept donations from people. He used the word "soup" to warn me that I would get into "hot soup" if I were to accept donations. As I have explained earlier, God uses everyday items and bodily gestures to communicate with me. Soup, for example, represents trouble ahead, and is God's way of warning me about potential problems so that I can avoid them.

All of this was from God; I depended entirely on Him, on His holy wisdom, vision and plans for the Church. I was full of joy, as I enjoyed the favor of the LORD. The Holy Spirit told me that God would "open the doors sharp" (meaning, in a wonderful way) for this church to be planted. I received holy wisdom from our Holy God, to employ a secretary to run the Church and to rent premises at the Bible House for church services. The church services would be conducted in both English and Chinese.

I also received holy wisdom from God as to who I could get to preach at the church services—Bible School students preparing to enter the ministry and overseas missionaries on short stopovers in Singapore. (By the way, the Spirit of God really loves these missionaries!)

I received further holy wisdom from the Holy Spirit, to reach out to Permanent Residents and foreigners in Singapore, as well as tourists visiting our country; the Church would be ministering to these people, but Singaporeans are also welcome to join us. All are welcome to volunteer their services at the various ministries in the Church. The Holy Spirit also encourages visitors to come to the Church for daily worship throughout the weekdays, in addition to attending services on weekends. Visitors coming for prayer or worship can bring along a stalk of rose as a symbol of their love for God, as they draw closer to the Spirit of God.

Worshippers will pray in tongues. They will all bow down to our Lord Jesus Christ and to our Holy God and to the Spirit of God during services. They will sing worship songs and receive visions from God. The Spirit of God loves to have worshippers swing and sway their bodies in a supernatural way, as they worship wholeheartedly in spirit, soul and body.

People who come to our services will experience the greatest presence on earth of our Holy God's kingdom. They will lift up their hearts and their hands, and worship the LORD in Spirit and in truth. As it says in the Bible:

> "God is spirit, and his worshippers must worship
> in the Spirit and in truth."
>
> *John 4:24 (NIV)*

I also received a vision from the Lord that this Church is to serve as a model for other churches which will be planted around the world. Tourists and foreign workers who visit my church will return home and plant churches in their own countries, using my church as a model. These churches will be a legacy for those who come after us—for it is God's will that they should be passed on from generation to generation.

CHAPTER 9

Obeying God—Even when I Am in Tears

God called me to write this book. Initially, I almost gave up because there were already so many good books in the market; but the Holy Spirit commanded me to obey, saying it was "His will" for me to write the book. Without His help, I would not have been able to do so; but God reminded me of many miraculous incidents I had already forgotten, so that they could be included in the book.

Where God commands, we must obey; for obedience is better than even the most extravagant sacrifice.

> "Has the Lord as much pleasure in your... sacrifices as in your obedience? Obedience is far better than

sacrifice. He is much more interested in your listening to him…"

1 Samuel 15:22 (TLB)

Once, when I was spending a few days at home, tears kept running down my face. I could sense the holy presence of God surrounding me. As I watched sermons on the internet, many times there were tears in my eyes. God's Spirit spoke to me, telling me that the Holy Spirit was present. I began to record down all that the Holy Spirit had done in my life. Although in the natural I had a bad memory, I started to recall incidents that I had long forgotten.

Memories kept flashing into my mind, clear and fresh as if the events had just taken place. The memories stayed in my mind until I had recorded everything down. (As I am not computer-savvy, I did an oral recording that was later transcribed by my daughter into written form.) It was the Holy Spirit who had worked this miracle, so that I could recall all the testimonies He wanted me to share with readers in my book.

As I embarked on writing the book, God showed me an image of tears and told me in advance that I would be writing the book "in tears". He did it to prepare me for the ordeal ahead of me. And it really happened just like He said. I am not fluent in English, so I struggled to find the right words to describe my spiritual experiences. I didn't know how to spell the words, and I couldn't write grammatical sentences.

I tell you the truth, I have not held a pen for decades until I started writing this book. From the time I was young until now that I am in my golden years, I have never written anything in my whole life, so I didn't know anything at all about writing a book. I cried over every word. It was painfully slow-going; it took me many hours just to write and rewrite, and then to check through the pages over and over again for mistakes I had made.

It was a very tough time for me. But I persisted because it was God's command to me to write this book. He gave me the strength to go on. God gives power to the weak. He made a way for me, where there seemed to be no way. Many times, the Holy Spirit would give me the words to write, or He would tell me to replace certain words I had written with more appropriate or powerful ones that He would give to me.

Slowly, the words became more and more until they grew into pages and the pages increased in number. The Holy Spirit kept reminding me of more and more testimonies to share, so much so that the number of pages kept on growing: at first, it was 10 pages; then the 10 became 20, increased to 30, and hit 40 pages—and still the memories kept pouring in, long-forgotten events that I would not have been able to recall on my own. Finally, the whole recording was completed at

60 pages of raw notes, to be rewritten into the actual stories for this book. I had begun writing in tears; but as I kept on writing, I began to experience God's peace, hope and joy. It was all God's doing; He alone made it all possible.

All this was done according to the Holy Spirit's timing, as I managed to finish the oral recording in time for my daughter to begin transcribing it just after she had passed her final-year university exams. What's more, she was able to complete the whole transcription before she got a job and started work!

While the work of writing and transcribing the book was going on, there was one occasion when God told me to check the transcript of my testimonies on the laptop. I had never used a laptop before and thought that I would have difficulties with it. But I obeyed. Wonderful! When I sat down, the laptop was already switched on and ready for me! All I had to do was simply to press the "up" and "down" buttons to read the contents of my book.

The Holy Spirit also showed me how I was to sell the book; I saw a vision of it being sold at a magazine stall. I also intend to sell the book online and to print flyers and banners advertising the book as well as the Spirit of God Christian church. The Holy Spirit has told me that this book is "salt" for the world—meaning that, like salt, it will benefit people, as their eyes will be opened to how they too can experience the Spirit of God moving actively in their lives.

As it says in the Bible:

> "You are the salt of the earth; but if the salt loses its flavor, how shall it be seasoned? It is then good for nothing but to be thrown out and trampled underfoot by men."
>
> *Matthew 5:13 (NKJV)*

Jesus, before I came to know you, I did not know that you cared so much for me. Now that I am saved, I am not ashamed to share the Gospel, although I did not even know how to write or where to start or what to do; but the Spirit of God gave me grace and holy wisdom. Therefore I rejoice that God's Spirit is with me and keeps me close to Him.

CHAPTER 10

Signs and Wonders from the Spirit of God

The Spirit of God never sleeps. He watches over me when I sleep. God's Spirit would wake me up whenever spirits came into my home. One night I woke up at midnight to see a spirit touching my nose. I called out, "Lord!" and the spirit disappeared.

The Spirit of God often appears to me as a transparent image in the form of a person, and we would talk together about many things.

God has opened my eyes and ears to discern the spirit realm. Things unseen and unheard by the physical senses, I have seen and heard with my spiritual eyes and ears. Everywhere I go, I see many people manifesting "cursed lights" inside them. A cursed light is a spirit living inside a human being, and it has a voice that speaks out of the person's body. I can hear the cursed light's voice talking to me, but the person and others around him will not be able to do so.

On another occasion, the Spirit of God woke me up at midnight. I started to pray in tongues. My voice sounded hoarse, as if I had a sore throat, but I continued to pray. A few nights later, God's Spirit again woke me up. I heard a voice praying in tongues. It sounded exactly like me when I was praying with a sore throat. God's Spirit opened my eyes to see a spirit praying in my living room.

Sometimes, when I am talking to a friend, I would smell a sweet fragrance that seems to be emanating, not from any physical object, but from the presence of the Holy Spirit. This is a supernatural aroma that can come from various sources. The Bible also refers to it on several occasions, such as the following:

> "For on My holy mountain, on the mountain height of Israel," says the Lord God, "there all the house of Israel, all of them in the land, shall serve Me; there I will accept them, and there I will require your offerings and the first fruits of your sacrifices, together with all your holy things.
> **"I will accept you as a sweet aroma** when I bring you out from the peoples and gather you out

of the countries where you have been scattered; and I will be hallowed in you before the Gentiles."

Ezekiel 20: 40-41 (NKJV)

Now thanks be to God who always leads us in triumph in Christ, and through us diffuses the fragrance of His knowledge in every place.

For we are to God the fragrance of Christ among those who are being saved and among those who are perishing.

To the one we are the aroma of death leading to death, and to the other the aroma of life leading to life. And who is sufficient for these things?

For we are not, as so many, peddling the word of God; but as of sincerity, but as from God, we speak in the sight of God in Christ.;

2 Corinthians 2:14-17 (NKJV)

Many times, too, as I walk along the streets, I begin to smell a familiar smell associated with my previous church. I look around me, but there is nothing that could have caused that particular smell. Then I begin to realize that it is the Holy Spirit who is supernaturally creating the smell to remind me of my previous church.

Once, I was on my way to see a doctor when I suddenly felt faint. I quickly sat down on the grass. At the time, I was suffering from diarrhea due to food poisoning. The Spirit of God opened my eyes to see a spirit pointing towards heaven. He was silently telling me that he was from heaven.

On another occasion, when I was visiting my father in hospital, I saw a spirit with food in its mouth, chewing vigorously.

On a separate occasion,, I was at a Traditional Chinese Medicine (TCM) clinic (I wasn't going for treatment there, just checking out their fees). The Spirit of God showed me the word "bread" out of nowhere. I went back to the place to look for bread.

One day, the Spirit of God moved my hand to cover my mouth; this means, "Don't talk" — that is, "Keep this matter a secret." Then He revealed to me that a member of my family had sinned against the Holy Spirit. As it says in the Bible:

> "He who is not with Me is against Me, and he who does not gather with Me scatters abroad. Therefore I say to you, every sin and blasphemy will be forgiven men, but the blasphemy against the Spirit will not be forgiven men.

> Anyone who speaks a word against the Son of
> Man, it will be forgiven him; but whoever speaks
> against the Holy Spirit, it will not be forgiven him,
> either in this age or in the age to come."
>
> *Matthew 12:30-32 (NKJV)*

The Holy Spirit said that this was a very serious matter, but I was not to talk to this family member about it. So I obeyed the Holy Spirit and kept quiet.

The Spirit of God has opened my spiritual eyes to see spirits talking with one another; to see an elderly man sitting in the sky and blowing a flute, as he floated across the sky. The Spirit of God has opened my eyes to see, in the atmosphere, many images of people's faces (these are faces of real people, such as my family, friends and famous people).

While taking a shower, dead cells started coming out of my back in a supernatural way, as I sensed the presence of God.

Once I was climbing up a ladder when I suddenly saw, on top of the ladder, a bright light. On another occasion, while in the course of delivering a document, I saw to my surprise that the consignment note I had taken back from the client had changed from white to blue; and that was when I again saw a bright light!

One day, I brought my dog to the veterinary clinic to be treated for a wound. While driving home from the clinic, I suddenly saw a spirit in the form of a woman. She was sitting beside me, pressing on the dog's wound. The dog barked once. I asked my daughter, who was with me, whether she had pressed on the dog's wound, and she said no.

Once, I was praying in tongues throughout the day, from 10 am till 5 pm. As I prayed, I was amazed to see the hairs on both my hands stand on end and begin to move in waves by themselves.

I saw a vision in the air; it was a vision of praying hands. I had a poster made, with a picture of those praying hands on it, together with quotations from my testimony. I could not put too many words on the plaque due to its limited space; but I still had a lot to say, so I have put my whole testimony into this book.

I wanted to have a cross made of marble with these words engraved on it: "Holy presence of God" in English and "Spirit of God Omnipresent Omnipotent" in Chinese. I worked on the computer, drawing up the design for the cross, and gave the design to the craftsmen who were making the cross for me. When they had completed the job, I displayed this Holy Cross in my home. It was a white marble cross with a red lining that ran all around the outer edge of the cross.

One night, at midnight, I saw that the red outer lining of the cross was flashing supernaturally. It normally does not shine in this way, but that night it kept on shining dazzlingly. I realized that God wanted to draw my attention to something about that cross. I checked on my computer and found that one of the Chinese words in my design had been missed out by the craftsmen; one word was missing from the marble cross! Nevertheless, the Spirit of God often uses that cross to speak to me.

On one occasion, I was facing the marble cross and looking at the Chinese words on it. I called out, "Spirit of God!" in Chinese, and the Spirit of God appeared to me. I will be putting this marble cross in the church that I am setting up, as I mentioned in Chapter 8 of this book.

CHAPTER 11

Snakes and Cursed Lights: a Warning about Evil People

*T*his is a true story that I witnessed with my own eyes: I saw a cell leader in my former church change into an evil man when he went against his pastor. This cell leader knew the Bible well, but he used Scripture—and even worship songs—for his own purposes. He challenged the pastor's stand on a particular matter, but the pastor stood upon his authority and told him, "This is the law." The cell leader insisted on fighting with the pastor over the issue, but the pastor refused to be drawn into the argument.

This cell leader had a "cursed light" (evil spirit) in him. If you don't like people with "cursed lights" (those with evil spirits in them), they will attack you and try to destroy you. When they talk, the best thing to do is to just keep quiet. The

Spirit of God said that everyone on earth is either for God or the devil. Evil people are heartless; they have no feelings or love for anyone but themselves. They cannot relate to others and they live only for themselves. They harden their hearts and refuse to listen to you; but *you* must listen to them. They reject what you say and try to block you from carrying out your plans. But in God there is freedom. Evil people do not like love, joy or peace.

> A good man out of the good treasure of his heart brings forth good; and an evil man out of the evil treasure of his heart brings forth evil. For out of the abundance of the heart his mouth speaks.
>
> *Luke 6:45 (NKJV)*

Evil people put on a false front of goodness to hide their true nature and hidden agenda. They are like wolves in sheep's clothing. The Holy Spirit said to me that evil people want to take away everything I have and destroy God's plans. The Bible has already warned us about such people:

> They come to you in sheep's clothing, but inwardly they are ferocious wolves. By their fruit you will recognize them.
>
> *Matthew 7: 15-16*

I have seen people close to me turning to evil. To begin with, I never had any problems with them; but when they became evil, they turned against me. Unaware of the change in them or the threat they posed to me, I continued to trust them.

Evil people will find your weakest points and use them against you. They will find a way to get close to you for their own evil purposes. First, they start by getting to know you well. Then they gain your trust by helping you. They show care and concern for you and then—suddenly, without any warning, they will make trouble for you. Their mindset is to serve the evil kingdom. Their lives are given over to stealing, killing and destroying, and their lives are controlled by evil. They talk with curses on their lips, and they live under a curse.

Evil people are connected with one another; they have eyes and ears everywhere, to tell them where you are going and what you are doing. They look for easy targets—for example, people with problems—whom they can get to join their evil kingdom.

> Love must be sincere. Hate what is evil; cling to what is good.
>
> *Romans 12:9*

The Spirit of God reveals to me what people are saying behind my back. I can catch, supernaturally out of the air, the very words they speak (just like what happened in 2 *Kings* 6, where Elisha knew what the king of Syria was saying privately in his own bedroom)—for example, someone was telling another person that there was nothing good for me and talking about other matters as well. *Thank you very much.*

> Now the king of Syria was making war against Israel; and he consulted with his servants, saying, "My camp will be in such and such a place." And the man of God sent to the king of Israel, saying, "Beware that you do not pass this place, for the Syrians are coming down there."
>
> Then the king of Israel sent someone to the place of which the man of God had told him. Thus he warned him, and he was watchful there, not just once or twice.
>
> Therefore the heart of the king of Syria was greatly troubled by this thing; and he called his servants and said to them, "Will you not show me which of us is for the king of Israel?"
>
> And one of his servants said, "None, my lord, O king; **but Elisha, the prophet who is in Israel, tells the king of Israel the words that you speak in your bedroom.**"
>
> *2 Kings 6: 8-12 (NKJV)*

The Holy Spirit tells me He has "tightened evil snake ghosts", meaning that He has prevented these evil people from harming me. The Spirit of God told me that there is pure evil everywhere today, in human beings and in the atmosphere. He has cautioned me that these evil people are big liars with powerful lying tongues; they never stand for Christ. Only those who stand for Christ and His Holy Spirit are true Christians. God told me not to talk to these "evil snakes"; that it is not worth my while to talk to them.

> "You snakes! You brood of vipers! How will you
> escape being condemned to hell?"
>
> *Matthew 23:33*

I have seen, right in front of me, human beings talking to a "cursed light" (an Angel of Light, evil spirit, or devil). The Spirit of God said to me that evil people listen to "cursed lights" and they have assignments from the Evil One. Because of the love of money, they have become evil. They have already lost their original human nature, and now they live in a purely evil way. As Jesus said, "[T]hey don't know what they are doing." (*Luke 23:34, NLT*)

There are some people who profess to be Christians, yet they love these "cursed lights". I once led a man to accept Christ as his Savior. He got baptized, joined a church cell group, was active in the church ushering ministry, helped the weak and went to church services regularly. Then I discovered he had put an idol in my van (I ran a courier service, and he was the deliveryman and driver of the van). When questioned, he replied that he was being secretly "monitored" by the evil kingdom (I don't know why).

There is no other way. If we want to live for Christ, we have to take up our cross and follow Him (*Matthew 16: 24-26*). The Bible tells us that nothing can separate us from God's love (*Romans 8:38*). So, choose to invest in heaven. As Jesus Himself has said:

> "No one can serve two masters. Either you will hate the one and love the other, or you will be devoted to the one and despise the other. You cannot serve both God and money."
>
> *Luke 16:13*

Some people believe that pain and problems come from "cursed lights" (evil spirits or the Evil One). It is true. The Spirit of God told me that it was a cursed light that was causing my body to be in pain and pulling out my teeth. But the Holy Spirit strengthens me with His supernatural power. Once, I felt a pain in my leg. There was no reason for it, as I had not injured myself in any way. I kicked away the pain from the cursed light, and it was gone!

Once, while I was having fish for dinner, I felt a sudden pain in my mouth. A small fishbone was poking into my gums. The Holy Spirit appeared to me (I saw His image) and said that the fishbone had been put there by a "cursed light" and that He would handle the problem for me. He did, and the fishbone miraculously disappeared without my having to do anything about it!

On another occasion, I asked the Spirit of God why I was "walking in the valley"—meaning, why I was facing so many troubles in my life at the time. He replied that those troubles were sent by a "cursed light". But our Holy God works all things out for my good. As it says in the Bible:

> And we know that God causes everything to work together for the good of those who love God and are called according to his purpose for them.
>
> *Romans 8:28 (NLT)*

CHAPTER 12

How the Holy Spirit Speaks to Me

$\mathcal{T}$he Holy Spirit speaks to me using everyday objects, common images and words, and simple bodily movements; each of these conveys a different and specific meaning. Below, I have given examples of each mode of communication. When the Spirit of God speaks, the message—in whatever form it comes—is always fresh, lively and full of supernatural power.

Using Objects to Communicate

This is the most common mode of communication. The Holy Spirit often draws my attention to an actual, physical object, and sometimes He will even turn my head around to look at it. For example, when He shows me a showerhead, He is calling me to pray. He will also show me what He wants me to pray for. When He shows me a piece of soap—which sounds like "soup"—He means "in hot soup"; that is, there are problems ahead or someone is in deep trouble.

Sometimes it is quite obvious what an object stands for. An umbrella, for instance, means "protection"; a money plant means "money"; a close-circuit camera means "eyes"; and fruit mean "the fruit of the Spirit". At other times, the object is used to convey a deeper and more specific message. For example, an electrical wire means "to be on fire for God"; and a wall plug means "plug in and act on it"; that is, to plug into the power of God and take action in a particular matter. When it is a power point with the switch in the "on" position, it means "take action"; if it is switched off, it means "relax; don't do anything".

A water pipe with a cover on it means that the Holy Spirit will "cover" (that is, protect) me when I am engaged in spiritual warfare with the enemy. A water-pipe joint, on the other hand, means that He will join in the fight with me and there will be a breakthrough. And when the Holy Spirit shows me a water tap, He is focusing on the word "tap" (as in tapping one's EZ-Link card at the train station entry and exit gantries, which allows the system to keep tabs on your travel movements) and telling me that He is keeping tabs on me.

When the Holy Spirit shows me a blank television screen that lights up, He means that "in the darkness you can see the Light". Light shining through the louvered glass panels of a small toilet window means that certain paragraphs of text (for example, in a book or periodical) will enlighten readers and cause them to see God. A clothespin—the kind that clips clothes together—means that someone has "clicked" (which sounds like "clipped") on a link directing them to my testimony on the internet.

The Holy Spirit often uses words that sound alike. For example, when He shows me a knife, He is telling me that someone—a particular person — is nice (which sounds like "knife"). A rusty lock, on the other hand, means "this is a nasty person". ("Nasty" sounds like "rusty"—get it?) A door means "this is a running dog"—in other words, a sycophant; but a ceiling fan means "this is a friend". ("Door" is close in sound to "dog", and "fan" to "friend".)

When the Holy Spirit shows me a cupboard handle, He means that He will handle a particular problem for me. When it is a shoe cabinet handle, it means that a particular organization is "handled" or run by "rats" (nasty people). And when the Holy Spirit shows me a shoe, He means "fool"; that is, He is warning me that someone is fooling me or about to fool me; or it can also mean that the person is a fool. A shirt collar, on the other hand, means "scholar"—indicating that this is a learned person.

When the Holy Spirit shows me a rice cooker, He is telling me, "This is Holy God's rice bowl" — that is, something extremely important or valuable to God, and dear to His heart. When He turns my head to look at the clock, it means that an event will take place "in God's timing". A hook means "hope"; and a document file means that He is telling me to "keep it"; for example, to file a piece of information away for future use. And when He shows me a packet of seeds, it means that I will be getting many new clients for my business. True! One by one, the clients kept coming to me!

A road sign, of an adult holding a child's hand, means that the Holy Spirit will hold my hand and walk with me. The Holy Spirit often uses road signs and other common signs to communicate with me. Here are some of them:

❖ A Pedestrian Crossing sign means that someone wants to "crossover";

❖ A "No Littering" sign means "don't throw away God's blessings" or "don't reject God's blessings";

❖ A "No Smoking" sign means "no spreading this piece of news around; don't talk about it";

❖ A hairdresser's "hair perm" sign means someone has been "burnt" or hurt by a past experience;

❖ A "No Parking" sign means "no barking" — that is, do not talk garrulously, like a dog barking noisily;

❖ A "No Dogs Allowed" sign means "no running dogs"; that is, "don't have anything to do with sycophants".

The Holy Spirit also gives me insights into people and information about them that I would not have known on my own. Here are some examples:

❖ A bird means "burst"; that is, someone can't hold it in anymore and is about to burst (for example, because of some strong emotion or exciting news);

❖ A box means "this is the boss";

❖ A button says "this is a pastor";

❖ A cat means "someone is scared";

❖ A key ring means "key person(s)"; for example, the board of directors or senior management of an organization;

❖ A lamp post or wall lamp means "a lamb" — that is, a good person

❖ A paper bag means "a batch of people";

❖ A shaving razor means that someone (a particular person) is safe and sound;

❖ A screw being tightened means someone is "tightening" his grip or control on another person;

❖ A sound speaker system refers to a "preacher";

❖ Paint means "pain" — that is, someone is in pain.

Sometimes the Holy Spirit uses everyday objects to show me what He wants me to do or to tell me about future events. The following are a few examples:

❖ A bottle of "Axe Brand" medicated oil means that the Holy Spirit wants me to take up cudgels and fight or protest against something;

❖ A bottle of Blanco (eraser fluid) means "don't write anything now";

❖ A chair means "better check this out";

❖ An eraser means "there is trouble ahead";

❖ A pencil or piece of paper means "write";

❖ A pendulum means "rise";

❖ A piece of tissue paper means "someone will do you a great favor".

Communicating through Images

Sometimes I receive visions and images in my mind when the Holy Spirit wants to communicate with me. For example, when He gives me an image of a postage stamp, it means that He wants me to take a stand on a particular matter. When He shows me a picture of weighing scales (the old-fashioned type, with two balancing pans), He is talking about justice.

A dove refers to the Holy Spirit and an image of angels means that there are angels present. A vision of an arrow means "shoot" — but not literally with an arrow; rather, it means "to shoot out words in a forthright way; to speak out strongly". A square shape—whether big or small—means "share sharp"; that is, to share the Gospel or my testimony deeply and in an excellent way with others.

On one occasion, the Holy Spirit showed me a vision of a lock on a bicycle wheel, to warn me that evil men were out to "lock" me up (that is, stop me) so that I could not do God's will, just like a bicycle that is unable to move if its wheels have been locked.

Revelations about People

Apart from using objects to give me insights into people, the Holy Spirit also gives me revelations about them by making me feel what they are feeling. When the Holy Spirit makes my heart beat very fast— in a way that is not natural, but supernaturally by His power—He is revealing to me that someone is scared. When He makes me feel a pain in my feet, again not naturally but by His supernatural power, it is a revelation from Him that someone is in pain.

Sometimes when I meet people, the Holy Spirit will reveal their true feelings to me, even when they try to hide them. When a person does not really like something (for example, a suggestion I make), the Holy Spirit will show me an unlighted bulb; but He will show me a lighted bulb if the person is happy.

Bodily Movements and Gestures

While I am fully in control of my own physical body, there are times when the Holy Spirit moves a part of my body—

usually one of my hands or legs—to give me a revelation about someone. For example, when He wants to show me that a particular person is feeling fearful, He moves my hand to scratch my ribs. When He is talking about what is in someone's heart—that is, what they are really like inside or what they are feeling—the Holy Spirit often moves my hand to scratch my chest.

When the Holy Spirit moves my fingers to dig my ears, He is telling me that someone has pricked up his or her ears (or has sharp hearing) and is listening attentively. When He moves my hand to scratch my head, He is indicating to me a particular person who heads an organization or is in charge of a certain project. And when the Spirit of God moves me to scratch my hand, He is informing me that someone "hangs" ("hand" sounds like "hang") — meaning, the person is in trouble or is paralyzed with fear because of a serious problem, much like a computer can't function anymore if it "hangs".

When the Spirit of God lifts my finger up to touch my eyebrow, He is telling me, "Holy God's rice bowl"—meaning that a particular matter is extremely important to God or close to His heart. And when the He moves my finger to plug my ear, He is telling me to listen attentively. Sometimes, the Holy Spirit makes my whole body go still; this is His signal to me to pause because He wants me to see something or He wants to reveal something to me.

When the Spirit of God moves my finger to rub my nose, He means that a particular person is from God. But if He lifts my finger to touch my lip, it means that what someone is saying is not from God —for example, a pastor preaching a sermon. It is only the person's own words (even though he may be claiming that it is a message from God). And when the Spirit of God moves my hand to touch the hairs on my chin, He is telling me that someone I am thinking of is safe.

When the Spirit of God moves my hand to make a clenched fist, with my thumb sticking out, and moves me to flick my thumb, He is telling me that a recent event is blessed and good. How blessed or good it is can be determined by the sound produced when my thumb is flicked.

When the Spirit of God knows that a blessing is coming my way, He would move my fingers to pinch my nose. When He wants to tell me that someone knows something about me, He would move my fingers to touch my nose sideways; if the person has important information about me, He would move my fingers to touch the middle of my nose. Breathing in deeply through the nose means there is a tough situation looming up ahead.

When the Holy Spirit raises my finger to touch my neck, He is telling me about "people in the nest" ("neck" and "nest" sound alike). This phrase refers to people who gather together for their own evil purposes and to talk maliciously about others, like a nest or brood of vipers. As it says in the Bible:

> You brood of vipers, how can you who are evil say anything good? For the mouth speaks what the heart is full of.
>
> *Matthew 12:34*

> They make their tongues as sharp as a serpent's; the poison of vipers is on their lips.
>
> *Psalm 140:3*

Words with Special Meanings

Sometimes the Holy Spirit speaks to me in words. Each word He uses holds a special meaning; for example, when He says "rest", He is telling me to be at peace and not to keep waiting anxiously for an event to happen.

The Holy Spirit often uses the word "sharp" to mean "knowledge that penetrates deeper into one's heart"; or "to seek or receive deeper knowledge, insight and discernment about a matter"; or "to do something excellently". For example, the Holy Spirit tells me that those who do me a favor "sharp" (meaning, in an excellent way) will be covered and have rest from trouble.

When the Spirit of God tells me that evil men want to "crucify" someone, He means that those people intend to destroy a particular person (who can be me or another person). The Spirit of God often tells me, too, that these evil people have set out to "crucify" (that is, destroy) God's work.

An "ape" or an "eight" means a person who prefers to please men rather than God. "Lamb", on the other hand, means someone who belongs to God's kingdom. "Ghost" means a spy (informer), or an evil person, or someone from the evil kingdom. For example, I have heard God's voice (an actual voice coming out of the air) telling me that it was not worth talking to "evil snake ghosts" — that is, it was not worth my time talking to devious schemers who were working for Satan.

Some other words that the Holy Spirit uses to communicate with me are:

- ❖ "Serve the Lord" means "serve the lost";

- ❖ "Comfort" means "a flock of sheep" — that is, the congregation in a church;

- ❖ "Central" means "sense it's real" — that is, it's genuine, not a fake;

❖ "Valley" means "trouble" (this word is used in the same sense as in *Psalm 23:4*, which talks about walking through the darkest valley);

❖ "Fish" means "available person" — that is, someone who is not a believer but is available for me to lead to Christ;

❖ "Chew" means to "keep chewing on and on" or to meditate on God's Word (the Bible);

❖ "Cursed Light" means an Angel of Light (that is, the devil) or an evil spirit. The Holy Spirit has told me that this "Cursed Light" wants to destroy God's plans but he is being "tightened" (see meaning below);

❖ "Tighten" means to hold someone tightly to prevent them from doing or saying something — for example, when the Holy Spirit tells me He has "tightened evil snake ghosts", He means that He has held them back from acting or talking against me. As I mentioned in Chapter 11 above, when people start to say negative things about me, God tightens His hold on them to shut them up.

Communicating with Numbers

Certain numbers convey specific messages from the Holy Spirit. Here are some examples:

- ❖ 00 means "No, no!"

- ❖ 1 means "eyes"

- ❖ 2 means "shoot and hook" or "shoot and hope"; that is, to "shoot" out words forthrightly, in the hope that the hearer is gripped or "hooked" by those words

- ❖ 3 means "heaven, earth and hook/hope"

- ❖ 4 means "false"

- ❖ 5 means "fight"; to challenge someone to a fight

- ❖ 6 means "fight" (see 5 above) and "hook" or "hope" (see 2 above)

- ❖ 8 or "ape" means someone who would rather please men than God

- ❖ 9 means "nice"

- ❖ 10 means "hang"

- ❖ 12 means "dwell"

Statement of Faith of Spirit of God Christian Church (Singapore)

Holy Spirit

We believe that the Holy Spirit was sent from God as life and power for those who believe in Jesus Christ. Through the Holy Spirit, we are transformed in our character and empowered in our services, so that we may be like Christ.

The Bible

We believe that the Bible is God's written Word. It contains all things necessary for salvation, teaches God's will for His world, and has supreme authority for faith, life, and the continuous renewal and reform of the Church.

Salvation

We believe that we are saved from our sins and reconciled to God only through believing and accepting what Jesus Christ has done for us on the cross. It is not by our efforts or merit, but it is a gift from God.

The Church

We believe:

❖ That the Church is the Body of Christ, whose members believe in Jesus Christ and acknowledge His headship. They are joined together by the Holy Spirit;

❖ The Scriptures, both Old and New Testaments, to be the inspired Word of God, without error in the original writings, the complete revelation of His will for the salvation of men and the divine and final authority for Christian faith and Life;

❖ In one God, creator of all things, infinitely perfect and eternally existing in three persons: Father, Son and Holy Spirit;

❖ That Jesus Christ is true God and true Man, having been conceived of the Holy Spirit and born of the Virgin Mary. He died on the cross, a sacrifice for our sins according to the Scriptures. Further, He arose bodily from the dead and ascended into heaven, where, at the right hand of the Majesty on High, He is now our High Priest and Advocate;

❖ That the ministry of the Holy Spirit is to glorify the Lord Jesus Christ and, during this age, to convict men, regenerate the believing sinner, and indwell, guide, instruct and empower the believer for godly living and service;

❖ That the true Church is composed of all such persons who, through saving faith in Jesus Christ, have been regenerated by the Holy Spirit and are united together in the Body of Christ, of which He is the Head.

Spirit of God Performs Miracles

Spirit God open eye show name card in van. Spirit God show water pipe dusty. Spirit God show plastic clothespin often speak in silent which means clip. Spirit God tell in silent show soap which means problem. Spirit God show Holy Spirit sign speak in silent which means Holy Spirit presence. Spirit God tell in silent like or don't like people. Spirit God tell in silent man of rush often. Spirit God tell in silent Holy God timing. Spirit God tell in silent cursed light. Spirit God call in silent to sell van. Spirit God call in silent to listen in presence.

Spirit God open spiritual eye seen unseen thing. Spirit God open spiritual eye seen spiritual person pray. Spirit God tell in silent before me in the presence. Spirit God open spiritual eye seen spiritual person point at heaven. Spirit

God know everything tell in silent. Spirit God appeared tell in silent in toilet about church fund. Spirit God tell in silent what you want self-service.

Spirit God tell in silent trust Holy God. Spirit God tell in silent evil man take away Holy God plan. Spirit God tell in silent online sermon pray in tongue is for me. Spirit God in me relationship deeper. Spirit God call in silent take Chinese tea. Spirit God with me in battle. Spirit God love overseas missionary. Spirit God tell in silent to write listen online sermon. Spirit God give knowledge and holy wisdom of God. Spirit God open spiritual eye seen bread English words in supernatural way appear out of nowhere.

Spirit God open spiritual eye seen fear no evil act in supernatural way. Spirit God show Angels sign speak in silent. Spirit God often tell in silent tighten. Spirit God tell in silent shoot in the track sharp. Spirit God tell in silent healing. Spirit God will tell in silent not from Holy God. Spirit God tell in silent supernatural tears flow. Spirit God tell in silent share sharp people said. Spirit God tell in silent hang.

Spirit God command in silent pray in tongue roll. Spirit God tell in silent Holy presence of God. Spirit God tell in silent need to go location bible house. Spirit God tell in silent evil man present. Spirit God tell in silent Holy God or evil. Spirit God open spiritual eye seen Holy God disappeared. Spirit God open spiritual eye seen Holy words. Spirit God open spiritual eye seen spirit in room. Spirit God make cough in present.

Spirit God teach what type preaching. Spirit God love body swing see Spirit God Holy spiritually appeared. Spirit God speak in silent powerfully his words. Spirit God cry out with tears solemnly. Spirit God often tell in silent crucify. Spirit God supernatural super power move head and open spiritual eye seen. Spirit God supernatural super power clenched fist with thumb sticking out. Spirit God tell in silent Nick Vujicic. Spirit God command in silent evil.

Turn head round from Spirit God. Bread from Spirit God. Spirit God command in silent his namesake for his people. File which means keep from Spirit God. No running dog from Spirit God. Spirit God turn my head see clock which means Holy God timing. Let us remember Holy presence of God from Spirit God. Spirit God command in silent listen radio.

Lighted bulb from Spirit God put out teeth from Spirit God. Switch on or off from Spirit God Spirit God command in silent. Mercy shall follow me. Spirit God command in silent paragraph. Supernatural super power stop write pen cannot write which means don't write unacceptable words stop by Spirit God. Spirit God used fingers to touch beard, which means safe. Spirit God picking nose, which means find out something. Spirit God scratched hands, which means hang.

Spirit God likes listen news, like degree people, Spirit God tell in silent sharp. Mortarboard/graduate hat which means degree or degree sharp. Spirit God love gospel and worshipping body swing. Believe this is bringing knowledge to life. beginning scared, Spirit God appeared tell in silent from Psalm poster fear no evil Spirit God appeared tell in silent from Psalm poster before me in the presence which means Spirit God inside body already before accept Christ.

Spirit God command in silent all the days of my life. Spirit God knows thoughts and responds to it immediately. Spirit God kept on talking about gospel even if don't understand. Crucify from Spirit God. Spirit God open spiritual eye seen spiritual person many other spirit. Spirit God act in supernatural way yawn tell in silent tired or don't want. Spirit God speak in silent protection over our family obedience better than sacrifice.

Spirit God open spiritual eye seen an elderly sitting in sky blow flute moved across sky. Spirit God teach sermon categorize. Spirit God show money plant. Spirit God supernatural super power wearing cross necklace dropped. Spirit God supernatural super power lift up finger touch nose eye brow lip face ear head. Spirit God tell in silent show wall got small hole. Spirit God kept reminding track broken.

Spirit God tell in silent about many things feedback about people reaction. Spirit God super power dynamic marvelous invisible. Spirit God let me know good or bad problem and other. Spirit God appeared tell in silent call him Spirit God. Anything from Spirit God perfect. Heart begging is to see the nation worship Spirit God. The HOLY LORD, The shepherd and his people from Spirit God. Spirit God command in silent all the days of my life.

Spirit God command in silent body half is Spirit God half is own hand and leg gestures talked in silent to each other. Spirit God often tell in silent evil men crucify. Spirit God tell in silent cursed light put pain in body pull out teeth. Spirit God turn head seen clock mean Holy God timing. Spirit God tell in silent cursed light want to take away Holy God plan. Spirit God tell in silent about evil enemy man of rusty and crucify.

Spirit God omnipresence omnipotent omniscient. Believe Spirit God in human life. Spirit God appeared I faced Holy cross look at Holy Chinese word call out name Spirit God. Spirit God tell in silent don't promise anything to worshipper. Spirit God appeared command in silent unacceptable donation. Reason soup which means problem. Spirit God tell in silent Holy presence of God. Spirit God open spiritual eye seen vision praying hands. Spirit God appeared presence seen face to face.

Spirit God appeared tell in silent fear no evil many other from Psalm poster. Spirit God supernatural Holy open spiritual eye seen heard Holy God voice speak alone, alone, alone and disappeared image saw Holy God image whole body was still only eye see lady voice . Spirit God tell in silent Holy Spirit presence. Spirit God command in silent the HOLY LORD the shepherd of his people.

Spirit God use hand cover mouth which means don't talk. Spirit God supernatural super power lift up finger touch eyebrow which means Holy God rice bowl. The Spirit God lives in me and commands in silent my body while fully in control of my own movements I nevertheless move according to his leading living lively actively in my life. Spirit God woke up to listen preaching on the internet.

At night was in master bedroom lie down on bed supernatural head turn one round seen up electrical wire track a bit scared and Spirit God tell in silent all go in to cupboard long sleeve and short sleeve hang Spirit God which means track are broken. Receive from Holy God Spirit God Christian Church. Spirit God kept reminding track broken tell in silent act in supernatural way. Spirit God opened eyes seen spirits talking in silent each other see spiritual person and others over time.

Spirit God opened eyes seen an elderly man sitting in sky blow flute moved across sky. Spirit God call in silent cut hair drink cold and hot healthy food many other praise the HOLY LORD faithful LORD. Spirit God released supernatural power wore cross necklace dropped on floor checked nothing wrong. Hearing from the HOLY LORD powerfully abide in his words. The HOLY LORD cry out with tears solemnly.

Spirit God tell in silent act in supernatural way super power people nose can smell about me.

Spirit God tell in silent cursed light have been tighten. Spirit God supernatural super power lift up finger touch small pimple pain beside nose which means someone checking pain act in supernatural way. Spirit God command in silent paragraphs to see light and Holy God words are sharp. Spirit God act in supernaturally way would categorize them under their respective ministries online.

Spirit God use gospel object words talk in silent presence living room. Spirit God turned head look money plant in toilet which means our conversation about money act in supernatural way. Spirit God teaching gospel use house hold all kind of object wall got small hole Spirit God tell in silent. Spirit God command in silent his namesake for his people. Holy Spirit command in silent daily office hour for worshipper to worship Spirit God only.

Spirit God call a person ape mean light. Act in supernatural super power my mind often dwell in gospel. Act in supernatural super power my mind keep on chew in gospel. Bible scripture "Let the word of Christ dwell in you richly in all holy wisdom, teaching and admonishing one another in psalms and hymns and spiritual songs, singing with grace in your hearts to the Lord." Colossians 3:16

Nevertheless, of those that chew the cud or have cloven hooves, you shall not eat, such as these: the camel, the hare, and the rock hyrax; for they chew the cud but do not have cloven hooves; they are unclean for you. Deuteronomy 14:7-9.

Receive hearing call Holy God. Spirit God tell in silent evil man crucify which means destroy. Pray or worship can bring along one stalk of rose more close to Spirit God for service. Tighten which means holy god hold a person movement or action or talking. Psalm 46:10: Be still, and know that I am God; I will be exalted among the nations, I will be exalted in the earth!

Revelation 19:15: Now out of His mouth goes a sharp sword, that with it He should strike the nations. And He Himself will rule them with a rod of iron. He Himself treads the winepress of the fierceness and wrath of Almighty God.

Isaiah 40:31: But those who wait on the Holy Lord shall renew their strength; they shall mount up with wings like eagles, they shall run and not be weary, they shall walk and not faint.

Fish which means available person. Neck which means someone in the nest. Spirit God supernatural super power lift finger touch my neck which means someone was in the nest. Sharp which means knowledge deeper in heart. Spirit God tell in silent evil men crucify which means destroy. Spirit God command in silent darkness can see light which means see God bible said Act 26:18 "to open their eyes, in order to turn them from darkness to light, and from the power of Satan to God, that they may receive forgiveness of sins and an inheritance among those who are sanctified by faith in Me."

I receive supernatural super power everywhere many people manifest spiritual idol mean light with voice speak in human body experience Holy God supernatural super power bible scripture "But you shall receive power when the Holy Spirit has come upon you, and you shall be witnesses to me in Jerusalem, and in all Judea and Samaria, and to the end of the earth." Acts 1:8 Hand which means hang. Touch my lip mean my own words. Chew which means chew the God's words on and on. Whole body still which means pause, valley which means trouble.

Holy God is a holy lady with voice speak to me part of angel. Spirit God supernatural super power lift finger touch my lip which means not from Holy God. I was writing the testimony and sit on the chair I don't know why seriously fell on the floor,. The chair was reverse. I feel supernatural super power landing very lightly on the floor and safe. at this moment, I speak out complete writing the testimony. Praise the lord. Holy God appeared is holy lady with voice speak to me part of angel.

Calendar bible words is Holy Spirit talk about my faith walk with the Lord. All act in supernatural way. Holy Spirit appeared talk to me in spiritually form of person image. Spirit God talk to me in spirit form image. I saw a spirit came into my home and ask what happen talk to the Spirit God and

Spirit God answer the spirit said it is the cursed light in the spiritually situation. Mark 5:41 "Holding her hand, he said to her, "Talitha koum," which means "Little girl, get up!""

I was riding the motorbike one of my hand was very numb Spirit God call for pray in tongue the numbness was gone praise the Lord. Presence with means sense. Atmosphere receive heard man voice speak in Chinese 天上无难事最怕有心人."Where there is a will, there is a way".

Because of my Chinese A5 book, Holy Spirit command power to know more with mean reader read to the testimony about God power to know more were go to new lever. Holy Spirit command bringing knowledge to life with means read the testimony know more about Holy God knowledge your faith go to new lever. Spirit God show words over with mean war is over. Holy God said lady voice is Holy God (confirm). Spirit God command reader to file or keep testimony.

Holy Spirit show the letter box window with means people close doors. Holy Spirit command many item show shine light. Holy God tell about spiritually power my hand muscle or place hand together pray for war was moving. Holy Spirit woke me up online sermon bible words for testimony thank you Lord. The book is not only for church fund also share the testimony to the whole world and fulfillment Holy Spirit his will.

Bible said Habbakuk 2:20 but the Lord is in His holy temple is for the name of daily worship. Bible said Luke 10:19

Behold, I give you the authority to trample on serpents and scorpions and over all the power of the enemy and nothing shall by any means hurt you. Bible said Joshua 1:9 for the Lord your God will be with you wherever you go.

I Heard the Voice of our Holy God

*E*xperience Holy God kingdom super power dynamic marvelous invisible. Obedience better than sacrifice. 1 Samuel 15:22. Atmosphere heard Holy God tell in silent fight matter. Atmosphere heard Holy Spirit command in silent a Chinese bible Matthew scripture 5: 3-10 calendar. Atmosphere heard Holy God step down. Atmosphere heard Holy God voice alone and disappeared. Atmosphere heard Holy God pass business to next generation. Atmosphere heard Holy God give room to girl. Atmosphere heard Holy God no need leave church. Atmosphere heard Holy God voice this is your church.

Atmosphere heard Holy God tithe. Atmosphere heard Holy God true Christian. Atmosphere heard Holy God plant church. Atmosphere heard Holy God don't go down stair eat. Atmosphere heard Holy God cancel personal thing. Atmosphere heard Holy God carrot juice. Atmosphere heard Holy God voice is lady speak. Atmosphere heard Holy God voice not worth to talk. Atmosphere heard Holy God seen vision tell in silent bow down and place hand together pray. Atmosphere heard Holy God worshipping with song in heart. Atmosphere heard Holy God voice and disappeared like throw stone in water spread out. Holy God know with part of body pain. Atmosphere heard the HOLY LORD, The shepherd and his people from Spirit God. Atmosphere heard Spirit God command in silent darkness can see light which means see God Act 26:18 "to open their eyes, in order to turn them from darkness to light, and from the power of Satan to God, that they may receive forgiveness of sins and an inheritance among those who are sanctified by faith in Me".

Atmosphere heard Spirit God command in silent all the days of my life. Atmosphere heard Holy Spirit command in silent this is bringing knowledge to life. Atmosphere heard Spirit God command in silent body half is Spirit God half is own hand and leg gestures talked to each other. Atmosphere heard Spirit God command in silent mercy shall follow me. Atmosphere heard holy wisdom from Holy God ministry for tourists and foreigners. Experience greatest Holy God kingdom lively actively presence on earth Holy Spirit, Spirit God, Angels, Holy God, Holy God words, HOLY LORD with me. Atmosphere heard voice Holy God said not worth talk to evil snake ghosts. Atmosphere heard Holy Spirit tell in silent tighten ghost snake evil. Atmosphere heard Spirit God tell in silent cursed light put pain in body pull out teeth. Atmosphere heard Spirit God tell in silent cursed light want to take away Holy God plan. Atmosphere heard Holy God kingdom tell in silent don't know or forgotten Holy words for The world power Testimony. Atmosphere heard Spirit God in human life. Atmosphere heard Holy Spirit command in silent the New Testament.

Atmosphere heard Spirit God appeared I faced Holy cross look at Holy Chinese word call out name Spirit God. Spirit God command in silent pray in tongue roll. Atmosphere heard Spirit God tell in silent don't promise anything to worshipper. Atmosphere heard Spirit God appeared command in silent unacceptable donation and fund. Reason soup which means problem. Atmosphere heard Holy Spirit command in silent his will Holy book. Atmosphere heard Spirit God tell in silent Holy presence of God.

Atmosphere heard Spirit God appeared tell in silent fear no evil many other from Psalm poster. Atmosphere heard Spirit God tell in silent Holy Spirit presence. Atmosphere heard Spirit God command in silent the HOLY LORD the shepherd of his people. Atmosphere heard Holy God dare spend money for LORD. Atmosphere heard Highly recommended from Holy God. Atmosphere heard Spirit God use hand cover mouth which means don't talk. Atmosphere heard Holy God use laptop check The world power Testimony. Atmosphere heard Holy Spirit command in silent Holy God open door sharp. Atmosphere heard Holy Spirit often to rest room tell in silent about cursed light or Holy God with bowel motion presence situation. Atmosphere heard Holy Spirit call in silent for abide in Holy God supernatural teeth were soft bite. Atmosphere heard Spirit God often don't like or unacceptable and not true presence situation caused fart. Atmosphere heard Holy Spirit call in silent for bible scripture put in The world power Testimony. Atmosphere heard Holy Spirit command in silent gospel lead deliver Holy words how to write. Atmosphere heard Receive holy wisdom from Holy God tithing and true Christian.

Atmosphere heard Holy God use me mightily shine for Jesus around The world. Atmosphere heard Holy God said brother against Holy Spirit. Atmosphere heard Spirit God finger plug in ear which means listen. Atmosphere heard Holy Spirit tell in silent trouble. Atmosphere heard Holy Spirit heal brain return memory receive holy wisdom from Holy God and health. Atmosphere heard receive Holy Spirit command in silent The world power testimony is salt which means "You are the salt of the earth; but if the salt loses its flavor, how shall it be seasoned? It is then good for nothing but to be thrown out and trampled underfoot by me" Matthew 5:13. Atmosphere heard receive holy wisdom from Holy God secretary run church Atmosphere heard receive Holy Spirit command in silent global Atmosphere heard receive Holy Spirit tell in silent God will make a way. Atmosphere heard receive Spirit God tell in silent need to go location bible house. Atmosphere heard receive Holy God voice alone came to pass take more than 10 years to know why. Atmosphere heard Receive from Holy God Spirit God Christian Church. Atmosphere heard receive Spirit God act in supernatural way super power that people nose can smell about me. Atmosphere heard receive Spirit God often tell in silent cursed light been tighten. Atmosphere heard receive from Holy God kingdom which means Holy book. Atmosphere heard receive Pray in tongue for healing spiritually warfare protection or prayer through Holy God with his power welcome Holy Spirit Holy presence supernatural tears flow. Atmosphere heard receive from the truth and the life I am your God. Atmosphere heard Spirit God command in silent his namesake for his people. Atmosphere heard Spirit God command in silent paragraph can see light which means see Holy God. Atmosphere heard receive from Holy God super power, Christian church, interesting to read, research, begging, step down, bible society, act in supernatural way. Atmosphere heard Holy Spirit command in silent share sharp. Atmosphere heard Holy Spirit command in silent rice bowl which means Holy God. Atmosphere heard Holy Spirit command in silent the power you know more. Atmosphere heard Holy Spirit command in silent open wing to fight which means challenging. Atmosphere heard Holy Spirit command in silent shoot go up mean raise. Atmosphere heard Holy Spirit appeared command in silent rice cooker which means Holy God rice bowl. Atmosphere heard Holy God rice bowl which means Holy God. Atmosphere heard Holy Spirit appeared command in silent worship the HOLY LORD in daily office hours. Atmosphere heard Holy Spirit appeared command in silent generation to generation planting new church. Atmosphere heard Spirit God call me in silent to pray in tongue for my hand numbness, at this moment my hand was very numbness was gone. Atmosphere heard Spirit God supernatural super power lift up finger touch eyebrow which means Holy God rice bowl. Atmosphere heard Holy Spirit holy calling open wings to shoot with angels with tears alone and justice. Atmosphere heard Jesus said I am the way the life and the truth. Atmosphere heard Spirit God supernatural super power destroy light bulb dead with sound bulb was on.

HOLY LORD powerful. Marvelous. Receive hearing call Holy God.

Holy Spirit Performs Miracles

*H*oly Spirit show super power invincible. Holy Spirit handle in trouble. Holy Spirit call in silent employ helper. Holy Spirit controlled handphone. Holy Spirit tell in silent do you favour sharp. Holy Spirit tell in silent trouble. Holy Spirit tell in silent God letters without s. Holy Spirit tell in silent hook in is cursed light. Holy Spirit tell in silent track draw line. Holy Spirit tell in silent track close door. Holy Spirit tell in silent war in presence. Holy Spirit sent to toilet. Holy Spirit tell in silent hold don't give.

Holy Spirit tell in silent Holy God open door sharp. Holy Spirit tell in silent face valley. Holy Spirit woke up listen online sermon. Holy Spirit make body itchy. Holy Spirit command in silent generation to generation plant church. Holy Spirit command in silent daily office hour worship the LORD. Holy Spirit command in silent Holy book cover words. Holy Spirit tell in silent evil lock God will. Holy

Spirit tell in silent wait upon the HOLY LORD for church. Holy Spirit is man appeared Holy Spiritually.

Holy Spirit tell in silent open wind pray. Holy Spirit tell in silent open wind shoot. Holy Spirit tell in silent open wind fight. Holy Spirit tell in silent God will make a way. Holy Spirit tell in silent protest. Holy Spirit tell in silent shoot go up. Holy Spirit tell in silent take healthy food. Holy Spirit tell in silent throw everything out you know. Holy Spirit command in silent file which means holy God The world power Testimony. Holy Spirit command in silent The new testament.

Real fresh from Holy Spirit. Abide from Holy Spirit. Spiritually fruit from Holy Spirit. 1.5 drinking bottle from Holy Spirit. Holy Spirit command in silent global. Holy Spirit command in silent see many people face light. The world power Testimony is salt which means "You are the salt of the earth; but if the salt loses its flavor, how shall it be seasoned? It is then good for nothing but to be thrown out and trampled underfoot by me" Matthew 5:13 from Holy Spirit valley from Holy Spirit war + war. Holy Spirit power stop talking control throat. Holy Spirit tell in silent receive power from Holy God. Holy Spirit tell in silent show pack of seed which means many new client obedience better than sacrifice. Holy Spirit tell in silent spiritually fruits. Holy Spirit command in silent this is bringing knowledge to life. Holy Spirit handle warfare trouble attack and many other.

Holy Spirit call in silent to send catholic theology. Holy Spirit supernatural power worshipping wept Holy Spirit super power dynamic. Holy Spirit tell in silent hot soup which means problem marvelous invisible. Holy Spirit talks about many things feedback about people reaction. Holy Spirit tell in silent Nick Vujick speak in church coughed is a light. Holy Spirit command in silent put scripture bible word in testimony anything from Holy Spirit perfect.

Holy Spirit let me know good or bad problem and other. Experience greatest Holy God kingdom lively, actively, presence on earth, Holy Spirit, Spirit God, Angels, Holy God, Holy God words, HOLY LORD with me. Holy Spirit tell in silent tighten ghost snake evil. Holy Spirit tell in silent Holy God were make a wave. Holy Spirit tell in silent ghost will make a wave. Experience Holy Spirit super power dynamic marvelous invincible. Holy Spirit tell in silent fishbone poke in mouth from cursed light Holy Spirit handle fish bone disappeared presence.

Experience Holy Spirit omnipresence omnipotent omniscient. Holy Spirit appeared presence seen face to face. Holy Spirit command in silent his will Holy book. Holy Spirit command in silent Holy God open door sharp. Holy Spirit often to rest room tell in silent about cursed light or Holy God with bowel motion presence situation.

Holy Spirit call in silent for abide in Holy God supernaturally teeth were soft bite. Holy Spirit call in silent for bible scripture put in The world power Testimony. Holy Spirit tell in silent trouble. Holy Spirit heal brain return memory receive holy wisdom from Holy God and health. Holy Spirit appeared command in silent many item got showed light. Holy Spirit appeared has commanded in silent that this book be named call The New Testament. Holy Spirit appeared command in silent join fight would be breakthrough. Holy Spirit appeared command in silent rice cooker which means Holy God rich bowl.

Holy Spirit appeared command in silent holding an axe sign which means protest. Holy Spirit appeared command in silent fruits which means spiritually fruits. Holy Spirit command in silent wait upon the HOLY LORD for the church. Holy Spirit command in silent spiritually fruits have purpose someone said don't know who. Hearing from the HOLY LORD powerfully abide in his words.

Holy Spirit command in silent provided memory to write how can Holy God harmony of idol. Holy Spirit act in supernaturally way tears weeping cough body swing. Holy Spirit prophesized example hot soup which means problem or sow many new client chosen someone to write testimony hold don't give all happened within a short period of time it true amazed. Holy Spirit command in silent visit mother pray her swollen leg until go back to Holy lord her leg fine. Contribute some money support mother Holy Spirit called in silent hold don't know why few months later go back to LORD.

When preacher preached powerfully strong words and serious abide in bible Holy Spirit tell in silent preacher have Holy Spirit and no running dog. Holy Spirit made body itchy could not sleep wake up online watch sermon act in supernatural way. Pray in tongue for healing spiritually warfare protection or prayer through Holy God with his power welcome Holy Spirit Holy presence supernatural tears flow the truth and the life I am your God.

Holy Spirit command in silent a Chinese bible Matthew scripture 5: 3-10 calendar "Blessed are the poor in spirit, for theirs is the kingdom of heaven. Blessed are those who mourn, for they shall be comforted. Blessed are the meek, for they shall inherit the earth. Blessed are those who hunger and thirst for righteousness, for they shall be filled. Blessed are the merciful, for they shall obtain mercy. Blessed are the pure in heart, for they shall see God. Blessed are the peacemakers, for they shall be called sons of God. Blessed are those who are persecuted for righteousness' sake, for theirs is the kingdom of heaven." Holy Spirit command in silent share sharp.

Holy Spirit command in silent rice bowl which means Holy God. Holy Spirit command in silent the power you know more. Holy Spirit command in silent open wing to fight which means challenging. Holy Spirit command in silent shoot go up mean raise. Holy Spirit appeared command in silent rice cooker which means Holy God rice bowl. Holy

God rice bowl which means Holy God. Holy Spirit appeared command in silent worship the HOLY LORD in daily office hours. Holy Spirit appeared command in silent generation to generation planting new church.

CONCLUSION

God Acts According to Your Belief in Him

*E*xperience God's kingdom living right now! Experience His dynamic, marvelous, SUPER power in your life! *It's possible; only believe!*

Believe that our Holy God is real and alive in heaven and on earth. Believe that He is a God of miracles, signs and wonders. Believe that with Him all things are possible. Believe that He answers your prayers. Believe that He has a plan for your life and that He directs your destiny.

God Himself commands us to believe in Him:

> And without faith it is impossible to please God, because anyone who comes to him must believe that

he exists and that he rewards those who earnestly seek him.

Hebrews 11:6

Believe in your Heavenly Father. Believe in His presence and in His supernatural power. Believe in His mercy and grace. Believe that He loves and strengthens you. Believe that He leads and guides you. Believe that He saves and protects you.

Believe that He is your Healer. Believe that He blesses you with hope, peace and joy. Believe, and receive holy wisdom, anointing, and all kinds of blessings from God!

Note to the Reader:

We invite you to share your response to the message in this book by writing to us at:
The World Power Testimony Books and Gifts
Email: lee_testimony@hotmail.com

Or visit us at:
http://tiny.cc/lee_gifts
Facebook page: lee_testimony
Testimony link: http://tiny.cc/lee_testimony

www.ingramcontent.com/pod-product-compliance
Lightning Source LLC
Chambersburg PA
CBHW031323040426
42443CB00005B/202